Simple Asset Allocation Strategies

Easy Steps for Winning Portfolios

by Roger C. Gibson
Foreword by Randal J. Moore
Introduction by Sir John Templeton

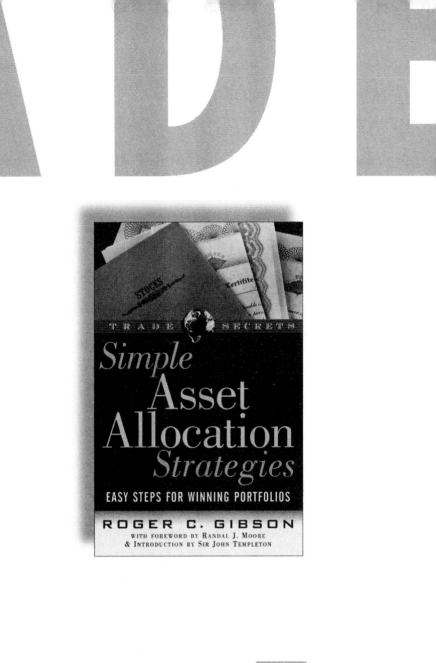

TRADE SECRETS

Simple **Asset** Allocation *Strategies*

EASY STEPS FOR WINNING PORTFOLIOS

ROGER C. GIBSON

WITH FOREWORD BY RANDAL J. MOORE
& INTRODUCTION BY SIR JOHN TEMPLETON

ISBN 1-883272-31-9

Printed in the United States of America.

Foreword

B y now just about every investment advisor has heard about Modern Portfolio Theory and Asset Allocation. It's a common topic at industry conferences. It's also hard to pick up a trade magazine that doesn't have an article on it. Yet, do you really feel that you have a firm grasp on what all of the excitement is about?

In *Simple Asset Allocation Strategies*, Roger Gibson shows investment advisors how to use the principles of Modern Portfolio Theory (MPT) to provide better investment advice to their clients. Gibson explains the importance of MPT in terms that can be understood by most advisors who possess a limited mathematical background. To keep it practical he also backs up many of his points with actual case studies of capital market behavior that confirm the principles of MPT.

The concepts of MPT are not new. Nearly 40 years old, the original work behind MPT was pioneered by Harry M. Markowitz in the 1950's in his work entitled *Portfolio Selection*. However, this is advanced academic work that is largely incomprehensible to practitioners. Roger Gibson explains the important principles of MPT in a clear and non-mathematical manner.

The use of portfolio optimization software to perform MPT calculations has grown with the interest in asset allocation. Interest in formalized Asset Allocation Modeling started in the insurance industry many years ago. Actuaries possessing extensive mathematical training would calculate the impact of changes in interest rates on insurance company assets and liabilities. Banks were also performing similar internal asset/liability studies.

Then, in 1974, with the passage of the Employee Retirement Income Security Act (ERISA), pension plan sponsors now had a legal requirement to document their investment decisions. Pension funds were to limit the investment risk in the fund to that taken by a "prudent man." Institutional funds now undertook formal diversification studies.

Beginning in the late 1980's, the concept of Asset Allocation began to reach the retail investment industry. New formulas were developed to handle the complicated tax planning issues faced by individual investors. The brokerage industry was changing and Asset Allocation was a concept that fit perfectly into the newly evolving investment industry paradigm.

At the same time, computer technology was becoming powerful enough to solve these problems on an advisor's desktop. Before 1990, most Asset Allocation modeling was performed on a centralized mainframe computer and users would access the program using an unreliable telephone and a modem. The process was slow and inefficient. The calculations (which are now instantaneous!) took an hour or more to finish. The cost of a typical study, which could take several months to complete, was many thousands of dollars.

The first developers of Asset Allocation software were true 'rocket scientists' whose attention had turned toward applying mathematical modeling to financial decisions. Irwin Tepper, Louis Kingsland and Henry Winklevoss, names mostly unknown by today's investment advisers, created the first commercial software applications in the early 1970's for analyzing asset allocation decisions. At first, the FORTRAN software was extremely sophisticated and nearly impossible for anyone but the original developer to use. Improvements in computer hardware and software programming have taken care of that.

As we come to the close of 1990's, the use of Asset Allocation software has grown beyond anyone's the wildest expectations. Earlier prognosticators felt that the arcane principles of MPT would never be palatable to the masses. Fortunately, these "visionaries" turned out to be wrong. The concepts that had now been successfully applied to institutional investment funds for over 20 years could add the same value to the portfolios of individual investors.

I founded Frontier Analytics in 1990 to provide PC-based Asset Allocation software to both retail and institutional investment advisors. Tens of thousands of investment advisors use our software to prepare asset allocation analysis for millions of portfolios.

We are pleased that Roger Gibson has helped educate investment advisors on the uses (and misuses) of Asset Allocation over the years with his excellent book *Asset Allocation: Balancing Financial Risk*. Now, in *Simple Asset Allocation Strategies*, Gibson turns his focus to the time horizon and the significant role it plays in evaluating the right asset allocation "mix" for each portfolio. He is truly an "asset" to our industry. Everyone can learn something by investing a few hours in reading this new primer.

Randal J. Moore
President
Frontier Analytics, Inc.
San Diego, California

Contents

Introduction

After 49 years of professional investment counseling worldwide, I believe that successful investing is mainly common sense. It is common sense to search for an asset where you can buy the greatest value for each dollar you pay. This means bargain hunting. For example, it is wise to compare a multitude of similar investments in order to select that one which can be bought for the lowest price in relation to other similar assets. If you buy a share of a company for a small fraction of its intrinsic value, then there is less risk of a major price decline and more opportunity for a major price increase.

To diversify your investments is clearly common sense so that those which produce more profits than expected will offset those which produce less. Even the best investment professional must expect that no more than two thirds of his decisions will prove to be above average in profits. Therefore, asset allocation and diversification are the foundation stones of successful long-term investing.

To diversify means that you do not put all of your assets in any one type of investment. Similarly, it is not wise to invest only in the shares of any one company, industry, or nation. If you search in all nations you are likely to find more good bargains and perhaps better bargains. Clearly you will reduce the risk because bear markets and business recessions occur at different times in different nations. Changing economic conditions also affect various types of investment assets differently. By diversifying among different types of assets, the value of your portfolio will not fluctuate as much.

To begin with modest assets and build a fortune obviously requires thrift. An investor seeking to become wealthy should adhere to an annual family expense budget that includes a large amount of savings. For example, during my first 15 years after college, I made a game of adhering to a budget that included saving 50 cents out of every dollar of earnings. Those who are thrifty will grow wealthy, and those who are spend-thrift will become poor.

Also, there is a magic formula called dollar-cost averaging in which you invest the same amount of money at regular intervals in an investment whose price fluctuates. At the end of the investment period, your average cost will be below the average price paid for the investment. In other words, your dollars will buy more shares when prices are low and fewer shares when prices are high, so that your average cost is low compared with the average for the market.

John D. Rockefeller said that to grow wealthy you must have your money work for you. In other words, be a lender and not a borrower. For example, if you have a big mortgage on your home, the interest paid will more than double the cost of the home. On the other hand, if you own a mortgage on a house, the annual interest on that mortgage will compound and make a fortune for you. If you never borrow money, interest will always work for you and not against you. You will also have peace of mind and be able to live through the bear markets and business recessions that occur in most nations about twice every 10 years.

It is only common sense to prepare for a bear market. Experts do not know when each bear market will begin, but you can be certain that there will be many bear markets during your lifetime. Common sense investing means that you should prepare yourself both financially and psychologically. Financially you should be prepared to live through any bear market without having to sell at the wrong time. In fact, your financial planning should provide for additional investment funds so that you can buy when shares are unreasonably low in price. Preparing psychologically means to expect that there will be many bull markets and bear markets so that you will not sell at the wrong time or buy at the wrong time. To buy low and sell high is difficult for persons who are not psychologically prepared or who act on emotions rather than facts.

When my investment counsel company began in 1940, on the front page of our descriptive booklet were these words: "To buy when others are despondently selling and to sell when others are avidly buying requires the greatest fortitude and pays the greatest reward."

Probably no investment fact is more difficult to learn than the fact that the price of shares is never low except when most people are selling and never high except when most are buying. This makes investing totally different from other professions. For example, if you go to 10 doctors all of whom agree on the proper medicine, then clearly you should take that medicine. But if you go to 10 security analysts all of whom agree that you should buy a particular share or type of asset then quite clearly you must do the opposite. The reason is that if 100 percent are buying and then even one changes his mind and begins selling, then already you will have passed the peak price. Common sense is not common; but common sense and careful logic show that it is impossible to produce superior investment performance if you buy the same assets at the same time as others are buying.

When selecting shares for purchase there are many dozens of yardsticks for judging value. A most reliable yardstick is how high is the price in relation to earnings. However, it is even more important to ask how high is the price in relation to probable earnings 5 to 10 years in the future. A share is nothing more than a right to receive a share of future earnings. Growth in earnings usually results from superior management. Even the best professionals have great difficulty in judging the ability of management. For the part-time investor, the best way is to ask three questions. Is this company growing more rapidly than its competitors? Is the profit margin wider than its competitors? Are the annual earnings on invested assets larger than for competitors? These three simple indicators will tell you much about the ability of management.

History shows frequent and wide fluctuations in the prices of many types of assets. Proper asset allocation helps to dampen the impact that these price swings will have on your portfolio. Asset price fluctuations may be even greater and more frequent in the future because all human activity is speeding up. This is one reason why you should not select a professional adviser based on short-term performance. For example, an adviser who takes the most risk is likely to have top performance in a bull market and the opposite in a bear market. Individual investors as well as managers of pension funds and university endowments should judge the ability of investment advisers over at least one full market cycle and preferably several cycles. This helps to balance out the element of luck and reveal which adviser has received the blessing of common sense.

I hope that almost every adult will become an investor. When I became an investment counselor there were only 4 million shareholders in America, and now there are 48 million. The amount of money invested in American mutual funds is now 1,000 times as great as it was 55 years ago. Thrift, common sense, and wise asset allocation can produce excellent results in the long run. For example, if you begin at age 25 to invest 2,000 dollars annually into your Individual Retirement Account where it can compound free of tax, and if you average a total return of 10 percent annually, you will have nearly a million dollars accumulated at age 65.

Investment management requires the broad consideration of all major investment alternatives. In this book, Roger Gibson develops the principles of asset allocation which make for good common sense investing in a rapidly changing world. In easily understood terms, he guides investment advisers and their clients step-by-step through a logical process for making the important asset allocation decisions. The broadly diversified investment approach Roger Gibson advocates should give investment advisers and their clients good investment results with increased peace of mind.

John M. Templeton,
Chairman of Templeton,
Galbraith & Hansberger

Part 1.

TIME HORIZON

He who wishes to be rich in a day will be hanged in a year. —
Leonardo da Vinci (1452-1519)
Notebooks, c. 1500

Money is of a prolific generating nature. Money can beget money, and its offspring can beget more. —
Benjamin Franklin (1706-1790)
Letters: To My Friend, A. B., 1748

Time is Archimedes' lever in investing. —
Charles D. Ellis
(1937- Investment Policy, 1985)

If you were charged with the task of dividing all the generally accepted and popular investment alternatives available into two groups on the basis of their investment characteristics, how would you do it? One way would be to rank them on the basis of their historical returns and look for a natural dividing line. With reference to the information in Table 1-1, we see that the biggest gap in historical returns exists between long-term corporate bonds and large company stocks. Using this as our dividing line, we would find that one group of investments would consist of Treasury bills, intermediate-term government bonds, long-term government bonds, and long-term corporate bonds-all of the interest-generating alternatives. The second group would consist of large company stocks and small company stocks-the equity alternatives with high historical returns.

Table 1-1
Total Returns, Income Returns, and Capital Appreciation of the Basic Asset Classes:
Summary Statistics of Annual Returns (1926 - 1994)

Series	Geometric Mean	Arithmetic Mean	Standard Deviation	Serial Correlation
Large Company Stocks:				
Total returns	10.2%	12.2%	20.3%	-0.01
Income	4.6	4.6	1.3	0.80
Capital appreciation	5.3	7.2	19.6	-0.02
Small Company Stocks:				
Total returns	12.2	17.4	34.6	0.09
Long-Term Corporate Bonds:				
Total returns	5.4	5.7	8.4	0.18
Long-Term Government Bonds:				
Total returns	4.8	5.2	8.8	0.08
Income	5.1	5.1	2.9	0.96
Capital appreciation	-0.4	-0.2	7.5	-0.06
Intermediate-Term Government Bonds:				
Total returns	5.1	5.2	5.7	0.27
Income	4.7	4.7	3.1	0.96
Capital appreciation	0.2	0.3	4.3	-0.09
U.S. Treasury Bills:				
Total returns	3.7	3.7	3.3	0.92
Inflation	3.1	3.2	4.6	0.64

Total return is equal to the sum of three component returns: income return, capital appreciation return and reinvestment return.

If we instead approached the task by ranking the investment alternatives on the basis of volatility as measured by their historical standard deviations, we would draw the natural dividing line in exactly the same place: between interest-generating investments and equity investments. Let us now contrast the investment characteristics of these two broad groupings.

An interest-generating investment is a loan that provides a return in the form of interest payments, with the promise that the principal will be returned at a stated maturity date. The primary advantage of this kind of investment is that the cash flows (interest payments and principal return) are specified in advance. The major disadvantage is that these investments tend to be very susceptible to inflation. Historically, interest-generating alternatives have not been capable of simultaneously producing an income stream while maintaining purchasing power.

By comparison, large company stocks and small company stocks are equity ownership interests in businesses. An equity investment provides return in the form of dividends and/or capital appreciation. It does not have a stated maturity nor is there any promise that the principal will be returned some day. But it also has no upper limit on its return possibilities. The primary advantage of an equity investment is the prospect for real (i.e., inflation-adjusted), long-term capital growth. The major disadvantage of an equity investment is the high short-run volatility of principal value.

In essence, these two broad categories, interest-generating investments and equity investments, represent the two alternate ways of putting money to work. It is the traditional distinction of being either a "loaner or an owner." A low return is the price paid by the "loaner" who wants the advantage of a more predictable outcome. Short-run volatility of principal is the price paid by the "owner" who wants the long-term capital growth possible with equities. This is simply an acknowledgment of the volatility/return relationship among investment alternatives. We previously discussed a wide variety of risks. In my judgment, however, the two most important money management risks are:

1. **Inflation** - which is most damaging to interest-generating
      investments.
2. **Volatility** - which is most pronounced with equity investments.

To focus our discussion, let us use Treasury bills as a proxy for interest-generating investments and large company stocks as a proxy for equity investments. In summary:

	Treasury Bills	Large Company Stocks
Advantage:	Stability of principal value	Long-term real capital growth
Disadvantage:	Susceptibility to inflation	Volatile returns

Given the higher returns produced by equity investments, one could conclude that investors have greater fear of stock market volatility than they have of inflation. This is evidenced by the lower returns they willingly accept with Treasury bills in order to have stable principal values. Many investors are overconcerned with the volatility of common stock returns and underconcerned regarding the damaging effects of inflation. There are several reasons for this.

First, inflation is insidious, taking its toll little by little over the long term. Second, investors who are not aware of the impact of inflation over time tend to view their investment results in nominal terms and generally prefer interest-generating alternatives. For example, during 1979 and 1980, when inflation reached a peak of 12 to 13 percent, Treasury bill returns were at a historical high of 10 to I I percent. Treasury bill investors tended to look at the accumulation of interest, ignoring that these high nominal returns were insufficient to compensate for the impact of inflation. Many investors still look at 1979 and 1980 as "the good old days" of high money market returns and deplore the lower, single-digit returns available as interest rates fell through the 1980s. Yet these investors were actually much better off in the lower interest rate environment. Returns were much higher in real terms then than prevailed during 1979 and 1980. It would be interesting to see how perceptions would change if Treasury bill investors had their returns routinely reported to them in inflation-adjusted terms.

Third, common stock volatility by comparison can do much more damage in the short run. On October 19, 1987, for example, we saw common stocks drop more than 20 percent *in one day*, compared with the highest recent *annual* inflation rate of 13 percent in 1979. Unfortunately, many investors focus too narrowly on the short term and incorrectly conclude that common stock losses are permanent. Some investors who suffered through the 1973-74 bear market for common stocks sold their equities near the bottom and therefore missed participation in one of the best bull markets in this century. In their discouragement they said to themselves, "Common stocks? - never again!"

In the short run, the possible negative consequences of stock market volatility will be much greater than the damage likely from inflation. Is the fear of common stock volatility warranted? In some circumstances it is, and in other situations, perhaps not. As we look into the future, there are two things we can count on. First, short-run common stock returns will remain unpredictable and volatile. Second, people will prefer predictability over uncertainty. For example, consider a choice between the following investment alternatives. Investment A has an expected return of 7 percent, with a standard deviation of 2 percent. Investment B has an expected return of 7 percent, with a standard deviation of 4 percent. Both investments offer the same expected return, but investment B has twice as much volatility as investment A. Rational investors are volatility averse. Given these alternatives, such investors will choose investment A. There is no incentive for bearing the higher volatility of investment B.

Economists refer to the "declining marginal utility of wealth" as underlying the explanation for this volatility-aversion. That is, each additional dollar that is acquired always increases one's well-being, but it does so at a declining rate. An extra 100 dollars means more to you if your net worth is 1,000 dollars than if you are a millionaire. In an investment context, this means that the additional dollar you make with a good outcome is not as valuable as the dollar that is lost with a bad outcome. In the real world, investors would sell investment B to buy investment A. By their doing so, the price of A would rise and the price of B would fall. In equilibrium, investment B would have a higher expected return to compensate for its greater volatility.

The same is true in our comparison of Treasury bills and common stocks. The buying and selling activities of investors in the marketplace cause common stocks to be priced to provide higher expected returns than Treasury bills, as compensation for bearing the volatility of equities.

In other work, I've presented evidence that indicated that market timing does not work. Consider what would happen, however, if there were an easy way to time the stock market. Investors would buy stocks in advance of a market rise and sell them in advance of a foreseen decline. This buying and selling activity, however, would change the pattern of future stock price behavior by smoothing out the market's ups and downs. There is only one problem: When common stock volatility disappears, so does the reward for bearing it! I therefore *prefer* a world where common stocks retain their short-run, unpredictable volatility. It is part of the foundation upon which their long-term higher returns are built. Implicit in the market timer's world view is the notion that money is made in common stocks *despite* the volatility. In contrast, the world view presented here rests on the notion that money is made in common stocks *because* of the volatility.

Now, the question becomes, "Under what conditions is the volatility worth assuming? "If we allocate the 6.5 percent equity risk premium across each of the 365 days in the year, we would find that the daily performance advantage of common stocks relative to Treasury bills practically disappears. On any given day, the chances are basically 50/50 that common stocks will outperform Treasury bills. Given the ever present volatility of common stocks, there is no incentive to assume equity risk on the basis of a one-day time horizon. The same is true for one month and one-year investments in common stocks. The standard deviation of large company stocks has historically been 20.3 percent. (Refer to Table 1-1.) This is much larger than the equity risk premium we expect to receive on average from holding common stocks. In the short run, although we expect to have higher returns in common stocks, the high volatility will swamp recognition of the equity risk premium. This is particularly troublesome for unsophisticated investors who often confuse this volatility for evidence of an irrational marketplace.

Time is one of the most important dimensions of the money management process. It is also often the least understood by investors. In assessing investment, alternatives, time horizon determines appropriateness. If it is known that an investor will need $20,000 next month to buy a car, a money market fund is a reasonable investment in the interim. A pension plan with known future nominal obligations (i. e., there's no provision for inflation-adjusted benefits) may decide to match the duration of those obligations with similar duration bonds or follow an immunization strategy.

Most longer-term investment situations, however, do not involve objectives with specific future nominal needs. There is simply too much uncertainty in the direction and magnitude of inflation. More often, the goal is therefore the preservation and/or accumulation of wealth in real terms. This requires the utilization of equity investments. Whereas in the short run we concluded that the volatility of equities is too great relative to the expected reward, this changes as the time horizon lengthens. For example, based on Ibbotson Associates' capital market data, from 1926 through 1994 large company stocks outperformed Treasury bills in 43 of the 69 years, or 62 percent of the time. If we compare the performance over longer holding periods of 5 years, 10 years, and 20 years, however, we find that large company stocks increasingly dominate Treasury bills 80 percent, 83 percent, and finally 100 percent of the time, respectively.

Assume for a moment that we have a stable inflation and interest rate environment. As the time horizon lengthens, the expected return from common stocks will not change, but the variability of holding period compound returns will decline dramatically. The longer the holding period, the more opportunity there is for good years to offset bad years, with the result that the range of compound returns converges toward the middle.

In Table 1 - 2, for example, comparisons are made among compound returns for large company stocks, long-term corporate bonds, long-term government bonds, Treasury bills, and inflation for 1-, 5-, 10-, and 20-year holding periods. In examining the information for 1-year holding periods, we see that in 39 of the 69 years (57 percent of the time) large company stocks outperformed the other three investment alternatives. But the returns ranged from -43.3 to 54.0 percent. Hence, although we expect large company stocks to outperform the other three investment alternatives in any given year, the penalty for underperformance can be quite high. The ranges of returns for other investment alternatives are narrower, as expected given their lower standard deviations.

As we stretch the time horizon to 10 years, large company stocks now dominate the other investment alternatives in 46 out of 60 periods, or 77 percent of the time. Not only has our confidence in being right with large company stocks increased, but the penalty for a bad outcome moreover is considerably less. The worst 10-year large company stock experience produced a compound average return of -.9 percent, On that basis, a $10,000 investment would have declined to $9,136 with full reinvestment of income. In 98 percent of the 10-year holding periods, the outcome was better than that!

Finally, we see that with 20-year holding periods, large company stocks outperformed the other three investment alternatives in 47 out of 50 periods, or 94 percent of the time. Although this is nearly 100 percent of the time, it is important to recognize that there have been three 20-year periods when

Table 1-2
Comparison of investment results for various holding periods (1926 - 1994)

	Large Company Stocks	Long-Term Corporate Bonds	Long-Term Government Bonds	Treasury Bills	CPI
69 One-Year Holding Periods					
Highest annual percent return	54.0	43.8	40.4	14.7	18.2
Lowest annual percent return	–43.3	–8.1	–9.2	0.0	–10.3
Number of periods with negative returns	20	16	19	1	10
Number of periods outpacing inflation	46	44	41	44	N/A
Number of periods with best of four returns	39	11	7	12	N/A
65 Five-Year Holding Periods					
Highest compound annual percent return	23.9	22.4	21.6	11.1	10.1
Lowest compound annual percent return	–12.5	–2.2	–2.1	0.1	–5.4
Number of periods with negative compound returns	7	3	6	0	7
Number of periods outpacing inflation	51	37	34	39	N/A
Number of periods with best of four returns	48	10	3	4	N/A
60 Ten-Year Holding Periods					
Highest compound annual percent return	20.1	16.3	15.6	9.2	8.7
Lowest compound annual percent return	–0.9	1.0	0.1	0.1	–2.6
Number of periods with negative compound returns	2	0	1	0	6
Number of periods outpacing inflation	53	31	27	33	N/A
Number of periods with best of four returns	46	8	0	6	N/A
50 Twenty-Year Holding Periods					
Highest compound annual percent return	16.9	10.2	10.1	7.7	6.4
Lowest compound annual percent return	3.1	1.3	.7	.4	.1
Number of periods with negative compound returns	0	0	0	0	0
Number of periods outpacing inflation	50	25	16	30	N/A
Number of periods with best of four returns	47	3	0	0	N/A

Source: *Stocks, Bonds, Bills and Inflation 1995 Yearbook.* © Ibbotson Associates, Chicago (annually updates work by Roger G. Ibbotson and Rex A Sinquefield). Used with permission. All rights reserved.

long-term corporate bonds provided returns superior to large company stocks. These were the 20-year periods beginning 1928, 1929, and 1930. The extreme market conditions accompanying the Great Depression were the cause of this unusual result. Although not shown in Table 1-2, if we stretched the holding periods to 25 years, we would find that large company stocks dominated the other three investment alternatives 100 percent of the time.

The volatility of common stocks is undoubtedly an enemy in the short run, but it is the basis for their higher expected return. Time transforms this short-run enemy into a friend for the long-term investor.

In Table 1-2 we noted that an investor's performance results will vary depending on the calendar year with which his holding period begins. Few clients, however, establish an investment position exactly at the beginning of a calendar year. The utilization of annual return data understates the range of returns for various holding periods. By changing the beginning point for various holding periods to a monthly rather than a calendar year basis, Figure 1-1 provides a more comprehensive comparison of the range of returns for Treasury bills versus large company stocks. The graph utilizes data from 1926 through 1994 and compares the range of returns for holding periods of 12 months (I year) to 240 months (20 years). Observe the potentially high penalty for being in large company stocks for holding periods as short as 12 months to 60 months.

As the holding period lengthens, however, the range of compound annual returns converges dramatically. Note that all 240 month holding periods had positive compound annual returns. It is also quite interesting to observe that the median return for large company stocks was approximately the same across the 12-, 60-, 120-, and 240-month holding periods. The median return for Treasury bills was, of course, much lower than for large company stocks, but was similarly relatively constant.

Figure 1-1, Large Company Stocks versus Treasury Bills: Range of Compound Annual Returns for various holding periods (1926 - 1994)

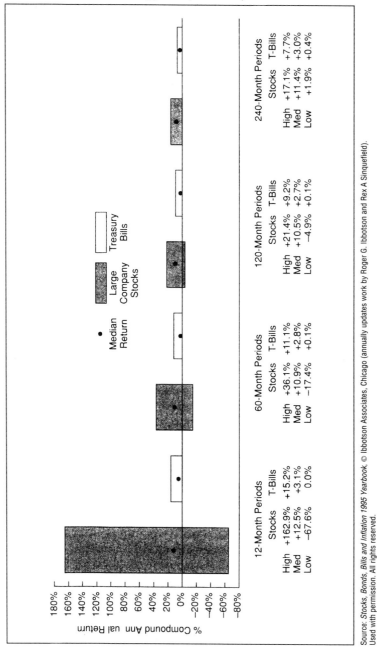

Source: *Stocks, Bonds, Bills and Inflation 1995 Yearbook*, © Ibbotson Associates, Chicago (annually updates work by Roger G. Ibbotson and Rex A Sinquefield). Used with permission. All rights reserved.

Figures 1-2A and 1-2B communicate the same message in a different form. Here, we can directly compare relative returns in a contemporaneous way for various holding periods. Again, we see that if stock market volatility is the disease, time is the cure.

The "miracle of compound interest" is also at work in the pattern of the increasing dominance of large company stocks over

Figure 1-2A, Large Company Stocks versus Treasury Bills: Compound Annual Returns for various holding periods (1926 - 1994)

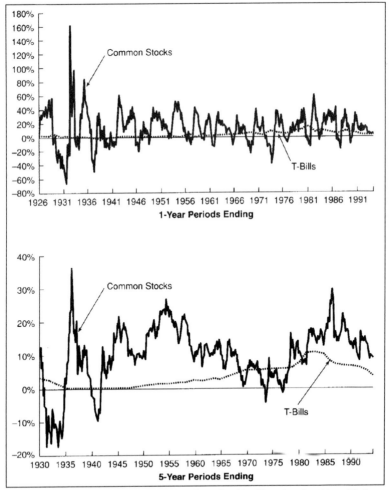

Figure 1-2B, Large Company Stocks versus Treasury Bills: Compound Annual Returns for various holding periods (1926 - 1994)

time. What seems like a modest 6.5 percent equity risk premium produces huge differences in wealth accumulation over long time periods. During the period 1926 through 1994, the 6.5 percent incremental return with large company stocks produced more than 66 times the wealth accumulation of Treasury bills. Assume Treasury bills now yield 6 percent, with the corresponding estimated compound return for large company stocks at 12 percent. In Table 1-3, we see that in only 13 years the cumulative wealth from an investment in large company stocks would double that of a corresponding investment in Treasury bills. By 20 years, large company stocks would be worth three times that of an investment in Treasury bills.

In summary, volatility swamps the expected payoff from common stocks in the short run, making them a risk not worth taking. But in the long run common stocks emerge as the winner, because of the convergence of average returns around common stocks' higher expected return, coupled with the miracle of compounding interest.

Table 1-3
Growth of $1 at interest

Years	5%	6%	7%	8%	9%	10%	11%	12%	13%
1	1.05	1.06	1.07	1.08	1.09	1.10	1.11	1.12	1.13
2	1.10	1.12	1.14	1.17	1.19	1.21	1.23	1.25	1.28
3	1.16	1.19	1.23	1.26	1.30	1.33	1.37	1.40	1.44
4	1.22	1.26	1.31	1.36	1.41	1.46	1.52	1.57	1.63
5	1.28	1.34	1.40	1.47	1.54	1.61	1.69	1.76	1.84
6	1.34	1.42	1.50	1.59	1.68	1.77	1.87	1.97	2.08
7	1.41	1.50	1.61	1.71	1.83	1.95	2.08	2.21	2.35
8	1.48	1.59	1.72	1.85	1.99	2.14	2.30	2.48	2.66
9	1.55	1.69	1.84	2.00	2.17	2.36	2.56	2.77	3.00
10	1.63	1.79	1.97	2.16	2.37	2.59	2.84	3.11	3.39
11	1.71	1.90	2.10	2.33	2.58	2.85	3.15	3.48	3.84
12	1.80	2.01	2.25	2.52	2.81	3.14	3.50	3.90	4.33
13	1.89	2.13	2.41	2.72	3.07	3.45	3.88	4.36	4.90
14	1.98	2.26	2.58	2.94	3.34	3.80	4.31	4.89	5.53
15	2.08	2.40	2.76	3.17	3.64	4.18	4.78	5.47	6.25
16	2.18	2.54	2.95	3.43	3.97	4.59	5.31	6.13	7.07
17	2.29	2.69	3.16	3.70	4.33	5.05	5.90	6.87	7.99
18	2.41	2.85	3.38	4.00	4.72	5.56	6.54	7.69	9.02
19	2.53	3.03	3.62	4.32	5.14	6.12	7.26	8.61	10.20
20	2.65	3.21	3.87	4.66	5.60	6.73	8.06	9.65	11.52
21	2.79	3.40	4.14	5.03	6.11	7.40	8.95	10.80	13.02
22	2.93	3.60	4.43	5.44	6.66	8.14	9.93	12.10	14.71
23	3.07	3.82	4.74	5.87	7.26	8.95	11.03	13.55	16.63
24	3.23	4.05	5.07	6.34	7.91	9.85	12.24	15.18	18.79
25	3.39	4.29	5.43	6.85	8.62	10.83	13.59	17.00	21.23

Time horizon is the key variable in determining the appropriate balance of interest-generating versus equity investments in a portfolio. This is summarized in the following comparison:

	Interest-Generating Investments	Equity Investments
Advantage:	Less volatility	Long-term capital growth
Disadvantage:	Inflation susceptibility	High volatility
Appropriate for:	Short time horizons	Long time horizons

Investors generally tend to underestimate their relevant time horizons. For example, consider new clients, husband and wife, both age 60, who when discussing their time horizon comment: "We both work now, but want to retire at age 65. Because we are only 5 years from retirement, our time horizon is very short. Equities were fine when we were young and building assets for retirement, but now that retirement is approaching, we should be cashing out of stocks to move into certificates of deposit and bonds, so that we can use the interest for living expenses during retirement."

This couple has confused their retirement horizon with their investment portfolio time horizon. The latter is much longer. If they plan to rely on their portfolio to support them through retirement, then their time horizon extends until the death of the survivor of them. For a man and woman of average health, both age 60, the life expectancy of the survivor of them is more than 25 years. As we have seen, over a 25-year time horizon, the danger of inflation is greater than the risk of common stock volatility, and accordingly equities should be meaningfully represented in their portfolio.

The tendency for investors to underestimate their time horizons leads to portfolios that are inappropriately underweighted in equities and therefore overexposed to inflation. This tendency is reinforced by the client's desire to measure performance over quarterly and annual time periods. Such measurement intervals are much too short to get a realistic assessment of progress toward the achievement of long-term objectives.

A proper understanding of time horizon as it relates to the investment process can dramatically alter a person's volatility tolerance. The next chapter builds a simple model for guiding clients in making the most important decision impacting portfolio performance: the balance between interest-generating and equity investments.

Part 2

A MODEL FOR DETERMINING BROAD PORTFOLIO BALANCE

Everything should be made as simple as possible, but not simpler —
Albert Einstein (1879 - 1955)

The client/adviser relationship begins with the data-gathering session. The purpose of this process is to get to know the client. Much of the information solicited is factual in nature and can be objectively determined. For personal clients, this information includes the value of assets and liabilities, sources of income and expenditures, tax situation, family composition, employment information, and so on. For institutional clients, such as qualified retirement plans or endowments, this information includes a list of investment positions, anticipated contributions and withdrawals from the portfolio, and a description of legal or regulatory constraints.

Another area of data gathering is subjective in nature and requires a more qualitative approach. This is the realm of client psychology, hopes and dreams, opinions and preferences regarding investments, and tolerance for various types of risk. Specifically, let us discuss the challenges involved in assessing the client's:

1. Specific goals
2. Investment objectives
3. Investment knowledge
4. Risks
5. Volatility tolerance

Chapter 2

SPECIFIC GOALS

Examples of goals for an individual money management client include:

- *Early retirement.*
- *College education for children.*
- *Buying a vacation home.*
- *Providing for an aging parent with declining health.*

For institutional money management clients, the goals might be to:

- *Provide retirement benefits to participants in a qualified plan.*
- *Fund the charitable pursuits of an endowment fund.*

When these goals are expressed, they often lack specificity. The adviser needs to help the client flesh out the goals in more detail. For example, does early retirement mean age 50, age 55, or age 60? What lifestyle does the client want in retirement, and what level of income will be necessary to sustain it? If the client wants to send three children to college, will they attend high-priced private institutions or less expensive public universities? Will scholarships be likely? Will the children get jobs in order to contribute to their own expenses? If the children are young, at what rate will tuitions rise in the interim?

Is a vacation home purchase a short-term or long-term goal? Approximately what price range is the client considering? What would be the expenses associated with a vacation home?

Does the client anticipate renting it when it is not in use? What kind of rental income could be obtained?

In the situation of the aging parent, is support presently being provided by the client? What sources of income does the parent presently have, and are there assets that can be sold to provide additional funds if needed? What kind of health insurance coverage does the parent have, and will he or she qualify for some form of government assistance for medical bills or income needs? Similarly, greater specificity can be developed for institutional clients who have quantifiable needs to fund future benefit payments.

Chapter 3

INVESTMENT OBJECTIVES

Once the client goals have been specified, the next step is to develop investment objectives that correspond to those goals. Much of this can be described mathematically in a relatively straightforward manner. Subject to reasonable assumptions, for example, we can calculate the annual investment necessary at a specified growth rate to accumulate a predetermined future sum of money.

Very often, however, client goals are more ambitious than can realistically be achieved. We have all had clients who decide to get serious about their retirement goals a few years prior to retirement. They are ready to modify their lifestyles as necessary to free up funds for investment in order to be assured a comfortable retirement. By that point, however, the lifestyle supportable at retirement has been largely determined. If the lifestyle is found to be seriously inadequate, there is probably little that can be done to materially improve it.

Human desires tend to exceed the resources available to fund them. In developing investment objectives, goals must therefore be prioritized and often compromised in the process of determining what is realistically possible in any given situation. Sound investment objectives are built upon realistic capital market assumptions and reflect the limitations of the client's available income and resources.

Chapter 4

INVESTMENT KNOWLEDGE

The best clients understand the general principles of money management and the characteristics of alternative investments. The long-term success of the investment management process depends to a large degree on the client's understanding of how his or her portfolio is structured and the manner in which it will behave. In the data-gathering process, it is helpful to have clients describe their good and bad experiences with investments. From their comments the breadth and depth of their knowledge can be gleaned. Often, advisers use questionnaires that exhaustively list many different types of investment alternatives. Clients are asked to indicate their familiarity with, preference for, and prior use of each investment alternative. I think it is important to recognize the primary purpose of such questionnaires and to be aware of their limitations.

A client who indicates on a questionnaire familiarity with, preference for, mid/or knowledge about common stocks, for example, does not necessarily, understand them sufficiently to make informed decisions regarding their use. At best, such questionnaires are a beginning point for an educational process that meaningfully involves the client. A -significant danger exists in inappropriately using the responses to such questions as a basis for either inferring volatility tolerance or choosing building blocks for constructing a portfolio. A client who says he has never invested in bonds and prefers not to use them may be only expressing unfamiliarity with them. It would be inappropriate to develop a portfolio excluding bonds solely on the basis of such a response.

By analogy, consider a person who consults a physician because of an ache or pain. The physician will not recommend a course of treatment based on the patient's familiarity with various prescription drugs. Investment preferences are often based on incomplete or erroneous information and should therefore not be used as the basis of a portfolio strategy or assessment of volatility tolerance.

Chapter 5

RISKS

In investment management, risk is often equated with the uncertainty (variability or standard deviation) of possible returns around the expected return. Clients, however, do not typically think in terms of expected return and standard deviation. More often, clients think of risk as it is defined in the dictionary: the chance of loss. Many investment counselors are in agreement that it is more accurate to think of investors as typically being "loss-averse" rather than "risk-averse." For example, the variability of returns investors experience from one year to another may not be particularly troublesome so long as there are no negative returns. Beneath the psychology of "loss aversion" lurks a conviction by some investors that negative returns represent permanent capital losses.

Another problem with loss-aversion psychology is that clients tend to think in terms of nominal rather than real returns. For example, many investors would feel better about earning 5 percent after taxes in a 12 percent inflationary environment than they would about losing 1 percent after taxes in a 4 percent inflationary environment. The positive nominal gain of 5 percent in this example creates the illusion of getting ahead, although adjusted for the 12 percent inflation, there is a real loss of 7 percent. In actuality they would be better off losing I percent in the 4 percent inflationary environment for a smaller real loss of 5 percent.

Many clients are fearful of equity investments. In working with them, the task is not to convert them from "risk avoiders" to "risk takers." As we concluded earlier, it is very rational to be risk-averse. Rather, the task is to sensitize the client to all the risks he or she faces, then to prioritize the relative dangers of these risks *given the context of the situation.* This is why we explored in detail the impact time horizon has on the investment management process.

It was only in reference to the relevant time horizon that we could determine whether volatility or inflation was the greater risk. For the long-term investor, volatility is not the major risk; inflation is. Because risk is time horizon-dependent, I will use the expression "volatility tolerance" when discussing the investor's ability to live with the ups and downs of investment markets. Although this may seem to be a subtle distinction, it is an important one. Occasionally, traditional investment terminology contributes to investor confusion. Although it is true that people prefer stability over uncertainty and therefore are "volatility-averse," it is not necessarily true that volatility is the major risk confronting the investor. Hence, it is a mistake to interchangeably use the words "risk" and "volatility." This distinction avoids the labeling of equity-oriented long-term investors as being risk takers! In my judgment, the equity-oriented investor with a long time horizon is following the *low-risk strategy* by holding a portfolio that offers protection from the biggest risk he faces—inflation!

Without guidance, most clients do not know how to realistically assess the risks they face. By default, they tend to assume that the familiar and comfortable path is the safe path, whereas anything unfamiliar or uncomfortable must be risky. For example, I have worked with a number of real estate professionals who consider themselves very risk-averse and fearful of common stocks. Yet, they are heavily invested in real estate (another equity) using high financial leverage. When the risk of such highly leveraged equity investing is pointed out to them, the response is often: "There's no risk there. I *understand* real estate and am *comfortable* with it!"

Chapter 6

VOLATILITY TOLERANCE

Investment advisers use a variety of methods to assess a client's ability to tolerate volatility. Given the problems we have discussed regarding using the terms "risk" and "volatility" interchangeably, it is obviously not advisable to simply ask clients to describe themselves as being either risk avoiders or risk takers. Given that choice, rational investors should answer that they are risk avoiders. The real issue is the amount of volatility that the client can tolerate. Some investment advisers look for volatility tolerance cues based on the client's business and personal lifestyles. For example, a person who likes the security of working for one employer for a lifetime and prefers recreational horseshoes may be more volatility-averse than a person who changes jobs relatively frequently in advancing his career and likes to parachute on the weekends.

The problems with these approaches are that they are highly subjective and are difficult to translate into a measurement of volatility tolerance. An examination of the client's current investment portfolio provides some clues but, again, the danger is that this may be more indicative of client familiarity and comfort with various investments than it is a measure of volatility tolerance.

Whatever approach is used to assess volatility tolerance, it is important to remember that it is not a fixed, inherited characteristic like blue eyes that stay blue for the rest of one's life. Accordingly, it is dangerous to develop an investment strategy on the basis of an initial assessment of volatility tolerance, regardless of how accurate the reading may be. To do so inappropriately presumes that clients already know what is in their best interest. If clients' risk perceptions are inaccurate, they cannot make wise decisions. Our task is to provide a frame of reference that enables clients to correctly perceive risks within the context of their situations. Surprisingly, a client's volatility tolerance can change within a rather broad range, based on an improved understanding of the investment management process. The informed modification of volatility tolerance is one of our major responsibilities to our clients and represents a great opportunity to add value. The modification of volatility tolerance often takes the form of clients becoming more comfortable with equity investments for long time horizons. In other situations, however, clients may gain increased awareness that the incremental return expected from common stocks is not sufficient to compensate for the volatility of returns if the investment time horizon is short. For these clients, volatility tolerance is appropriately lowered with a corresponding reduction in equity investments as their perceptions become more realistic.

Chapter 7

THE PORTFOLIO BALANCE MODEL

Admittedly, there is a gap between the money manager's world of "expected returns and standard deviations" and the client's world of money without taking risks!" The first part of this book is devoted to a discussion of the long-term historical performance of various investment alternatives. On the basis of this information, we developed simple models to estimate the long-term compound annual returns and risks as alternatives. As we guide clients through this capital market review, their perceptions and expectations become more realistic and their capacity for making improved investment decisions develops. Without this process, few clients are equipped to make the right decisions for themselves.

The most important decision that the client makes deals with the allocation of portfolio assets between interest-generating investments and equity investments. This decision determines the basic volatility/return characteristics of the portfolio and quantifies both the likelihood of reaching investment objectives and the range of possible outcomes. A methodology is needed that forces the client deal realistically with the tradeoff between volatility and return. The model we will develop uses simplistic assumptions. Although some rigor may be lost in this simplicity, the effectiveness of the model should ultimately be judged by the criterion of whether it effectively helps the client to understand the volatility/return trade-off. If the client makes better decisions and more confidently adheres to investment policies, the model accomplishes its purpose.

In the first chapter, we divided the investment world into two categories: interest-generating investments and equity investments. We concluded that each category has a primary advantage and disadvantage. Interest-generating investments provide promises regarding payment of interest and principal, but are susceptible to purchasing power erosion as a consequence of inflation. By contrast, equity investments have historically been able to build purchasing power through capital growth, but have the disadvantage of high volatility.

To highlight these differences, we chose Treasury bills as a proxy for interest-generating investments in general and large company stocks as a proxy for the wide variety of equity investments. We concluded that the appropriateness of Treasury bills versus large company stocks was primarily determined by the investment time horizon. For long time horizons, inflation poses a larger risk than stock market volatility, and accordingly a portfolio should be oriented more heavily toward common stocks and other forms of equity investments. For short time horizons, stock market volatility is more dangerous than inflation, so portfolios should be more heavily positioned in Treasury bills and other interest-generating investments that have more predictable returns.

By adding the historical equity risk premium of 6.5 percent to the Treasury bill yield, we derived an estimate of the future compound annual return for large company stocks. Given the high volatility of common stocks, we also know that the realized equity risk premium will vary widely. (Refer to Figure 7-1, which shows the historical volatility of the equity risk premium on a rolling five-year basis.) Unfortunately, the actual equity risk premium is not subject to direct measurement.

Some forecasters use macroeconomic models to try to predict the equity risk premium with greater accuracy. This, of course, presumes that the careful analysis and manipulation of macroeconomic data can provide a unique insight missed by the capital market participants as a whole—a very difficult achievement in highly efficient markets. Other forecasters eval-

Figure 7-1
Equity Risk Premium (1926-1994)

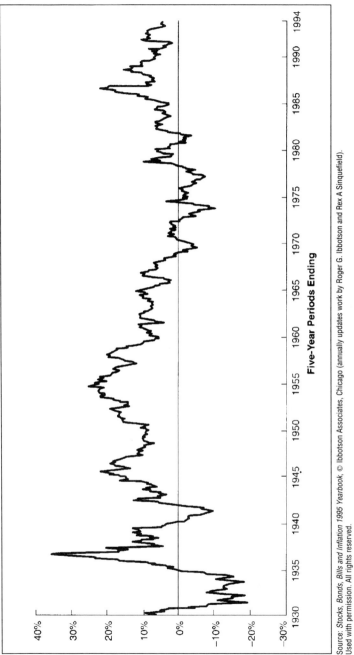

uate the current economic environment and attempt to find similar conditions at other times in history to develop a better prediction of how the capital markets may behave. For example, if there is a concern regarding the prospects of accelerating inflation, historical returns are examined from other periods of history where accelerating inflation was experienced. This selective use of history presumes that we can correctly determine in retrospect what caused the markets to behave as they did and that current market behavior will be determined by the same causal relationships. Again, this is quite difficult to do successfully.

The easy way out may also be the best way out. This is to simply assume that the historical equity risk premium of 6.5 percent is a reasonable estimate of what the equity risk premium should be. This has been the historical reward received for bearing equity risk, based on a long time horizon encompassing periods of both war and peace, economic expansions and contractions, high and low inflation, Republican and Democratic administrations, and so on. There will always be unusual events, and arguably an estimate built on the basis of long-term experience may be the safest approach. The precision of this estimate of the equity risk premium is not particularly important for two reasons. First, in the short-run, the high standard deviation of common stock returns will always swamp recognition of the expected equity risk premium. So whether the actual equity risk premium is 6 percent or 7 percent makes little difference. Second, the purpose of the methodology is not to derive accurate estimates of expected returns, but rather to develop a systematic way of making broad portfolio balance decisions that acknowledge the volatility/return trade-off.

Let us discuss the steps involved in our methodology for guiding clients in making this most important investment policy decision affecting portfolio performance.

Step 1: *Verify that your client fully understands the volatility/return characteristics of Treasury bills and large company stocks.* (Refer to Table 7-1.)

Table 7-1, Volatility/Return Characteristics of Treasury Bills versus Large Company Stocks

Expected Return	Volatility*	Comments
Treasury Bills		
6%	±0%	The expected return of 6% is the yield on a one-year bill as shown in *The Wall Street Journal*. The volatility is shown as ±0% because the return can be locked in with no uncertainty.
Large Company Stocks		
12%	±20%	The expected return of 12% is derived by adding the historical equity risk premium of 6% (rounded to the nearest percentage) to the current Treasury bill yield of 6%. The volatility of ±20% is the historical standard deviation of returns for large company stocks from 1926 through 1994.

* There are two chances out of three that the actual return will be in a range defined by the expected return plus or minus the volatility.

Step 2: *Review with your client the importance of time horizon in assessing risks and evaluating the appropriateness of interest-generating investments vs. equity investments.*

Step 3: *Determine the current value of your client's total investment portfolio. This includes:*

A. All liquid and illiquid investments (e.g., investment real estate) even though the latter cannot be easily converted to cash.

B. The value of employer-sponsored retirement plans, even though the client may not have investment discretion of the funds.

C. The present value of annuitized streams of income. Although these are not normally thought of as invest ment assets and are seldom reflected on the balance sheet, they are nevertheless important economic assets that should be considered in structuring portfolios.

This third step helps the client to think of his or her portfolio in the broadest terms and focuses the attention on the "big picture."

Step 4: *Instruct your client to hypothetically convert his or her entire investment portfolio to cash.* This conversion overcomes inertia by freeing the client from the ghosts of past investment decisions.

Step 5: *Describe a hypothetical investment world where there are only two investment alternatives Treasury bills and large company stocks. Ask your client to allocate the cash from his or her liquidated investment portfolio between these two alternatives.* In doing so, the client should keep in mind the volatility/return characteristics of each alternative and his or her relevant investment time horizon.

In reviewing the range of choices available to the client, consider a portfolio composed entirely of Treasury bills. Of all possible alternatives, this portfolio has the lowest expected return. This is the price paid for the elimination of short-run volatility. As we begin to allocate money to large company stocks, the volatility of the resulting portfolio increases in direct proportion to the percentage invested in these stocks. Table 7-2 shows the volatility/return characteristics of five portfolios ranging from 100 percent Treasury bills through 50 percent Treasury bills/50 percent large company stocks to 100 percent invested in large company stocks.

Table 7-2, Example of portfolio choices

	Portfolio Balance		Expected Portfolio Performance		
	Treasury Bills	Large Company Stocks	Expected Return*	Volatility*	Typical Range of Results**
1	100%	0%	6%	±0%	6%
2	67	33	8	±6.7	1.3% to 14.7%
3	50	50	9	±10	−1% to 19%
4	33	67	10	±13.3	−3.3% to 23.3%
5	0	100	12	±20	−8% to 32%

Investment decisions are made under terms of uncertainty. For this reason, it is better to forecast portfolio results in terms of typical ranges around expected returns. For example, rather than simply saying portfolio 2 has an expected return of 8 percent, it is much more meaningful to indicate that the likelihood is two chances out of three that the actual result will be within plus or minus 6.7 percent of the expected return of 8 percent. This implies a typical range of results from 1.3 to 14.7 percent.

Clients bring to the client/adviser relationship their own expectations regarding the expected returns and volatility associated with various investment alternatives. Often, clients believe that returns are more easily achieved with less volatility than indicated here. Such clients struggle with the portfolio choices presented in Table 7-2. If so, that is good. If there is going to be a struggle over the nature of the volatility/return trade-off, it is best to deal with it at this point in the process. Generally, clients will accept the framework because the alternative requires the rejection of nearly seven decades of historical relationships in favor of a different investment world view.[1]

By dividing the 20 percent standard deviation of large company stocks by the 6 percent presumed equity risk premium, we see that for every 1 percent increase in the portfolio's expected return, portfolio volatility will increase by plus or minus 3.3 percent. For example, portfolio 2 has two-thirds of its asset in Treasury bills, with one-third in large company stocks, and has an expected return of 8 percent. In order to increase the expected return by only 2 percent more, we need to shift an additional one-third of the portfolio out of Treasury bills into large company stocks. Doing so, however, increases portfolio volatility by an additional plus or minus 6.6 percent!

---

[1] It should be noted that on a portfolio basis using multiple asset classes, incremental returns are possible with less volatility than this simple "two-investment alternative world" implies. In working with clients, however, it is better to avoid holding out such hope at this point in the decision-making process.

Awareness of this trade-off forces the client to focus more attention on his ability to tolerate short-run portfolio volatility. This process is healthy because in determining overall portfolio balance it is more important to concentrate on volatility tolerance than on return requirement. Most clients require unusually high rates of return to achieve all of their goals. These high rates of return often are not possible given reasonable capital market expectations. Even if they are possible, they should not be pursued unless the client has both the objective and subjective capacity to tolerate the associated volatility.

Having reviewed the historical performance of the capital markets, a client should have developed an awareness that the higher returns from equity investments are the compensation one expects to receive in exchange for the volatility assumed. A client's volatility tolerance, in this framework, is simply the added volatility he is willing to accept in exchange for an extra unit of expected return. If the return associated with a client's maximum volatility tolerance is insufficient to realize his goals, he should either modify his goals or acknowledge that they will most likely not be realized. If the return associated with the upper limit of his volatility tolerance is more than is needed to accomplish his goals, it is easy to move down to a more stable portfolio if that is his preference.

Psychologically, it is easier to tolerate volatility if the final outcome occurs in the distant future. A proper understanding of time horizon, therefore, increases volatility tolerance for the long-time-horizon investor. Unfortunately, however, the liquidity of the capital markets provides constant revision of security prices and a heightened awareness of short-run performance. The trick is to avoid attaching too much significance to short run performance numbers if the relevant outcome is truly associated with a long-term time horizon.

Table 7-2 by itself may be sufficient for use by those clients who have a good, intuitive grasp of the impact that the passage of time has on narrowing the range of portfolio com pound returns. Other clients may need to have the range of returns over time for each portfolio specified in more detail.

Figure 7-2, Portfolio 1, Growth of $1

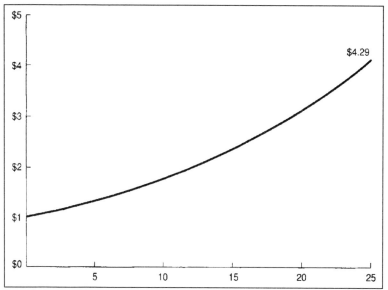

Figure 7-3, Portfolio 2

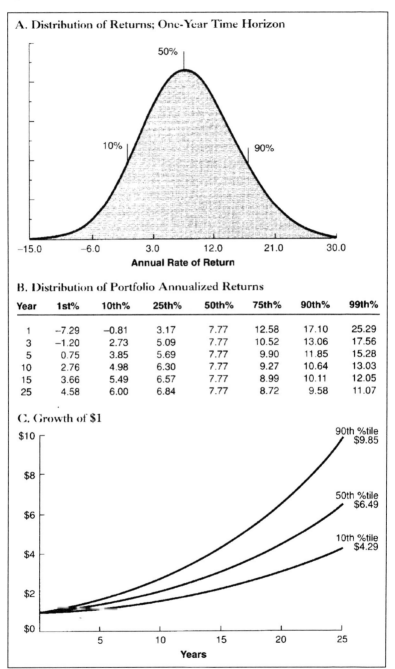

A. Distribution of Returns; One-Year Time Horizon

50%

10% 90%

| -15.0 | -6.0 | 3.0 | 12.0 | 21.0 | 30.0 |

Annual Rate of Return

B. Distribution of Portfolio Annualized Returns

Year	1st%	10th%	25th%	50th%	75th%	90th%	99th%
1	-7.29	-0.81	3.17	7.77	12.58	17.10	25.29
3	-1.20	2.73	5.09	7.77	10.52	13.06	17.56
5	0.75	3.85	5.69	7.77	9.90	11.85	15.28
10	2.76	4.98	6.30	7.77	9.27	10.64	13.03
15	3.66	5.49	6.57	7.77	8.99	10.11	12.05
25	4.58	6.00	6.84	7.77	8.72	9.58	11.07

C. Growth of $1

$10

90th %tile
$9.85

$8

50th %tile
$6.49

$6

10th %tile
$4.29

$4

$2

$0

| 5 | 10 | 15 | 20 | 25 |

Years

Source: *Stocks, Bonds, Bills and Inflation 1995 Yearbook,* © Ibbotson Associates, Chicago (annually updates work by Roger G. Ibbotson and Rex A Sinquefield). Used with permission. All rights reserved.

38 Simple Asset Allocation Strategies

Figure 7-4, Portfolio 3

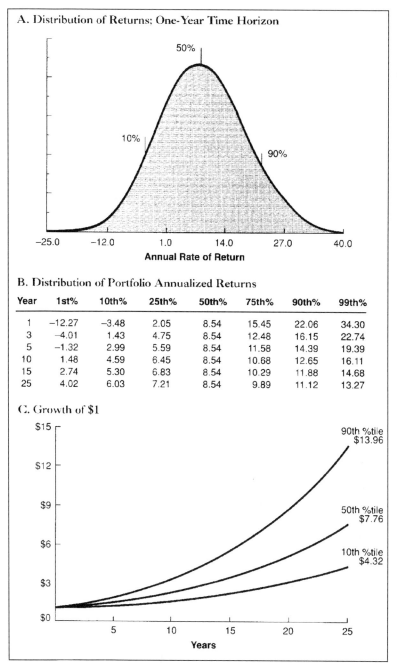

A. Distribution of Returns: One-Year Time Horizon

B. Distribution of Portfolio Annualized Returns

Year	1st%	10th%	25th%	50th%	75th%	90th%	99th%
1	−12.27	−3.48	2.05	8.54	15.45	22.06	34.30
3	−4.01	1.43	4.75	8.54	12.48	16.15	22.74
5	−1.32	2.99	5.59	8.54	11.58	14.39	19.39
10	1.48	4.59	6.45	8.54	10.68	12.65	16.11
15	2.74	5.30	6.83	8.54	10.29	11.88	14.68
25	4.02	6.03	7.21	8.54	9.89	11.12	13.27

C. Growth of $1

Figure 7-5, Portfolio 4

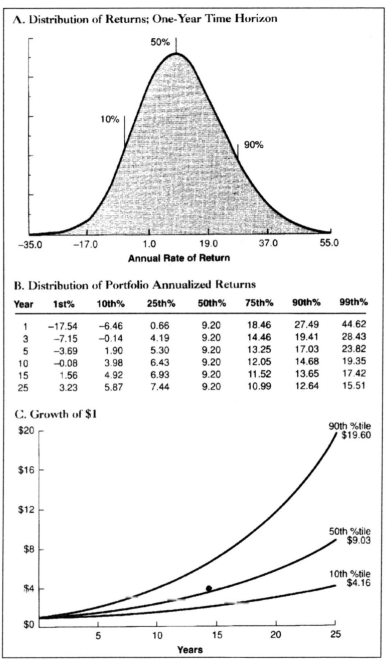

A. Distribution of Returns; One-Year Time Horizon

50%

10%

90%

| -35.0 | -17.0 | 1.0 | 19.0 | 37.0 | 55.0 |

Annual Rate of Return

B. Distribution of Portfolio Annualized Returns

Year	1st%	10th%	25th%	50th%	75th%	90th%	99th%
1	-17.54	-6.46	0.66	9.20	18.46	27.49	44.62
3	-7.15	-0.14	4.19	9.20	14.46	19.41	28.43
5	-3.69	1.90	5.30	9.20	13.25	17.03	23.82
10	-0.08	3.98	6.43	9.20	12.05	14.68	19.35
15	1.56	4.92	6.93	9.20	11.52	13.65	17.42
25	3.23	5.87	7.44	9.20	10.99	12.64	15.51

C. Growth of $1

$20

90th %tile
$19.60

$16

$12

50th %tile
$9.03

$8

10th %tile
$4.16

$4

$0

| 5 | 10 | 15 | 20 | 25 |

Years

40   Simple Asset Allocation Strategies

Figure 7-6, Portfolio 5

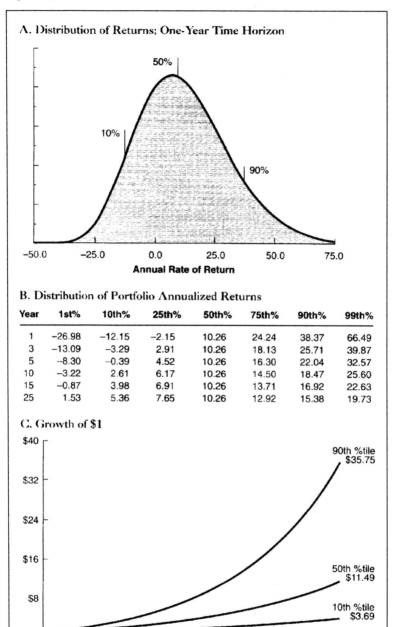

A. Distribution of Returns; One-Year Time Horizon

50%

10%

90%

-50.0	-25.0	0.0	25.0	50.0	75.0

Annual Rate of Return

B. Distribution of Portfolio Annualized Returns

Year	1st%	10th%	25th%	50th%	75th%	90th%	99th%
1	-26.98	-12.15	-2.15	10.26	24.24	38.37	66.49
3	-13.09	-3.29	2.91	10.26	18.13	25.71	39.87
5	-8.30	-0.39	4.52	10.26	16.30	22.04	32.57
10	-3.22	2.61	6.17	10.26	14.50	18.47	25.60
15	-0.87	3.98	6.91	10.26	13.71	16.92	22.63
25	1.53	5.36	7.65	10.26	12.92	15.38	19.73

C. Growth of $1

$40

$32

$24

$16

$8

$0

90th %tile
$35.75

50th %tile
$11.49

10th %tile
$3.69

5	10	15	20	25

Years

For them, Figures 7-2 through 7-6 can be used in conjunction with Table 7-2 to communicate the impact time has on the choice of portfolio balance. For those who like graphs, the distribution of returns for a 1-year time horizon is shown in Figures 7-3A through 7-6A for portfolios 2 through 5. No such distribution is shown for portfolio 1 because it has a fixed annual return of 6 percent. Figures 7-3B through 7-6B show in tabular form the "distributions of portfolio annualized returns," which describe the likelihood of achieving various returns over 1-, 3-, 5-, 10-, 15-, and 25-year time horizons. Finally, Figures 7-2 and 7-3C through 7-6C show the path of wealth accumulation over time for each of the five portfolios for the 10th, 50th, and 90th percentile compound return probabilities.

As we review the distribution of portfolio annualized returns for portfolio 3 in Figure 7-4B, we see that -3.48 percent is shown at the 10th percentile for a 1-year time horizon. This means that there is a 90 percent likelihood that the actual return will be higher than -3.48 percent and a 10 percent likelihood that it will be lower. Under the 10th percentile column for a 5-year time horizon, however, we see a value of 2.99 percent. That is, there is a 90 percent likelihood that, for a 5-year holding period, this portfolio will have a compound annual return in excess of 2.99 percent. For a 25-year horizon, there is a 90 percent likelihood that the compound annual return will be greater than 6.03 percent-an interesting outcome when one considers that the return available from Treasury bills is 6 percent. As expected, with longer time horizons there are more opportunities for good and bad years to offset each other, thereby narrowing the range of outcomes. Under the 25th percentile column we find a value of 2.05 percent for a 1-year time horizon. That indicates that the chances are three out of four that the portfolio return will exceed 2.05 percent over a 1 year time horizon, and so forth.

If we compare portfolio 2 with portfolio 3, we will find that the median (50th percentile) return is lower and that the range of possible outcomes for any comparative time period is correspondingly less for portfolio 2. By contrast, portfolio 4 will have wider ranges of outcomes with a correspondingly higher median (50th percentile) return.[2]

A comparison of these exhibits shows the variation in short-run volatility based on the percentage of the portfolio allocated to large company stocks. It also clearly demonstrates that the passage of time dramatically narrows the range of compound returns for each portfolio. This is consistent with the conclusions reached in Chapter 1, which dealt with the importance of time horizon.

Investment objectives are usually solicited from clients during the initial data-gathering session. Occasionally, a client will express an objective of "12 percent compound returns with little or no risk," which qualitatively translated would be "very high returns with stable principal values." This is not one investment objective; it is two competing objectives, and to the extent to which one objective is pursued the other must be sacrificed. This is simply the volatility/return trade-off implicit among the choices in Table 7-2.

We now have an appreciation of the necessity of educating your clients and providing them with a context for making good decisions. According to Charles D. Ellis, portfolio-balance decisions are investment policy decisions, which are the non-delegatable responsibility of the *client*. Within the framework developed, the client's choice of a portfolio from Table 7-2 is an indirect measure of the client's *informed* volatility tolerance.

This model is not without its drawbacks. The notions of expected return and standard deviation are not well understood by most clients. For this reason, the model has been

---

[2] With a normal distribution, the range of returns is symmetrically distributed around the expected return. In reality, security returns are better described by a lognormal distribution which has a longer right tail. This is because it is impossible to lose more than 100% of your money, but the upside is open-ended. With a "right-tailed" lognormal distribution, the range is not symmetrically distributed around the expected return. The graphs and tables in Figures 7-3 through 7-6 utilize the more realistic lognormal distribution assumption.

designed to be as simple and straightforward as possible. There is also a risk of the choices being too hypothetical and therefore not realistic to clients. This can be overcome by incorporating discussions of historical capital market experiences like the 1973-74 bear market, when common stocks lost more than 40 percent of their value. Such market declines have occurred in the past and will surely happen again in the future. Clients should be educated to expect that.[3]

This exercise for determining broad portfolio balance should be engaged in periodically with clients. Over time, their experiences with investments will change and their reactions may differ from what was initially expected. For example, some clients who thought they thoroughly understood common stock volatility and could live with it may temper their opinions following a stock market crash like that of October 1987. Various life events can also occur that alter volatility tolerance. Examples are changes in family composition, job or career changes, or health problems.

Through these changes, this decision-making model will continue to emphasize the fact that to increase expected return, one must willingly accept increased volatility. The balance chosen between interest-generating investments, as represented by Treasury bills, and equity investments, as represented by large company stocks, is the most important investment decision the client will make. It determines simultaneously the volatility and return characteristics of the portfolio. Subject to this basic policy decision, the adviser can proceed to design a more broadly diversified portfolio, utilizing multiple asset classes.

---

[3] Another dilemma with the model is that, technically, the standard deviation should be measured around the arithemetic average return rather than the compound return. To use the arithmetic return in the model, however, may mislead the client into thinking that his money will compound at that rate. (Note: the arithmetic return will always be higher than the corresponding compound return for a variable pattern of returns). Use of the compound return number avoids this problem. In my judgment, the technical inaccuracy serves the more important consideration of the client's conceptual understanding. Within a time-horizon context, clients will naturally think of compound returns, yet their experience of volatility will be in the near term.

Part 3:

Investment
Resource
Guide

▲ ▲ ▲ ▲ ▲

Tools for
Investment
Success

Getting Started in Asset Allocation
by Eric Gelb & William Bresnan
An indispensable new guide for all planners and advisers.
Covers all the basics of asset allocation including: Practical
guidelines and sound advice for implementation; Important
asset allocation techniques; Determining financial objectives &
cash flow needs;Tactical asset models; Mutual funds and asset
allocation; balancing portfolios and much more.A comprehensive new gem.
288 pp $18.95 Item #T135x-10517

The New Money Management
by Ralph Vince
Introducing a remarkable asset allocation system that brings an
easy-to-follow rigor to previous models of investment selection
and timing. Learn to accurately measure the benefits and consequences of a trade before committing to it - which dramatically increases your odds for success.
$65.00 Item #T135x-2835

Wealth Management (IAFP): *The Financial Advisor's Guide to Investing and Managing Your Client's Assets*
by Harold R. Evensky
The "Dean of Financial Planning" gives detailed coverage of the
process for setting up a wealth management program dedicated to the goals and lifestyle of the client, rather than any particular investment.Also highlights modern investment theory,
asset allocation, portfolio optimization and investment policy,
plus secrets for attracting new clients, managing their expectations and establishing workable investment plans.
$50.00 Item #T135x-3552

Thriving As A Broker In The 21st Century
by Tom Dorsey

A top adviser and money manager presents the ultimate guide for brokers who want to get ahead now and in the coming years. He show brokers how to shape their practices; how to build a strong, enduring client base in light of new competition from the Internet, mutual funds, retail banks and others. Includes interviews with the industry's top rung: Ed Rosenberg of Paine-Webber, Dennis Nelson of Piper Jaffrey and more. A "must-have" new manual.

$39.95 Item #T135x -10540

Global Asset Allocation: *Techniques for Optimizing Portfolio Management*
by Jess Lederman & Robert Klein

Spotlights the most promising portfolio management strategies in use today for institutional investors to minimize risk and maximize returns. From asset liability forecasting and target asset allocation to the critical time horizon and implementing overlay strategies, this working handbook is designed to help professionals make decisions and solve the real-world problems they encounter.

$69.95 Item #T135x-6074

Tax-Smart Investing
by Andrew Westhem & Stewart Weissman

This new bestseller guides financial planners through the mine field of tax consequences of a wide range of investment vehicles and offers practical and proven methods to minimize the tax burden of investment earnings. Based on years of expertise in this arena, Westhem's latest work is a great tool for financial planners to review as they evaluate the best investment vehicles for their clients.

$49.95 Item #T135x-10583

The Management of Investment Decisions

by Trone, Allbright & Taylor

The first step-by-step guide to the entire investment consulting process. Incorporates modern investment management theory and legal elements of fiduciary conduct. It outlines management techniques followed successfully by huge pension funds and foundations - all explained in simple, usable concepts. From objective goal setting, asset allocation and investment policy statements to implementation and performance monitoring, you'll find 5 steps of the investment process needed to achieve investment objectives and avoid fiduciary liability.

$65.00 Item #T135x-6207

Prudent Investment Guide to Beating the Market

by Reinhardt, Werba & Bowen

Asset class investing has never been more critical to portfolio returns - and now it's easy to understand and implement. By refining and implementing time tested concepts of Modern Portfolio Theory, the authors show how to create a "scientifically" balanced, or efficient, portfolio, attracting large returns without assuming additional risk levels.

$30.00 Item #T135x-3418

FP Books - www.fpbooks.com - The #1 source for financial planning and investment books, videos, software and other related products. Find the most thorough selection of new releases and hard to find titles geared towards financial planners, advisors and anyone managing and investing money today.

Frontier Analytics - www.frontieranalytics.com - Established in 1990, Frontier Analytics an investment technology firm dedicated to developing Windows-based investment analysis software for retail and institutional professional investors worldwide. Frontier Analytics develops and markets several of the leading portfolio management software programs that are used in the financial services industry. Over 15,000 retail and institutional professional investors worldwide rely on its programs, including banks, securities brokerage firms, accounting firms, insurance companies, plan administration firms, money management companies and independent fee-based consultants.

International Association for Financial Planning -

www.ctiafp.com - A professional membership association dedicated to two guiding principles: 1) Everyone needs objective advice to make smart financial decisions; and 2) The financial planning process is the foundation for smart decision making. Members of the IAFP are individuals and companies who sign a code of professional ethics and are committed to using the financial planning process to help people achieve their financial goals. A variety of disciplines and backgrounds are represented among members of the IAFP, including financial advisers, accountants, attorneys, trust officers, stock brokers and insurance professionals.

National Association of Personal Financial Advisors (NAPFA) - www.napfa.com - NAPFA is the largest professional association of comprehensive, fee-only financial planners in the U.S. The association has more than 640 members and affiliates in 50 states. In addition to providing members an opportunity to network and exchange practice management information, NAPFA actively promotes public awareness of comprehensive Fee-Only financial planning.

The Institute of Certified Financial Planners (ICFP) - www.icfp.com - The ICFP is a professional association of more than 15,000 CFP© licensees and candidate members nationwide. Members adhere to a code of ethics, continuing education and disclosure requirements in the interest of providing the highest level of professional service to their clients. Headquartered in Denver, CO, the Institute provides benefits to Certified Financial Planner (CFP) licensees nationwide. Benefits include consumer assistance, publications, and local chapters.

MAGAZINES & PUBLICATIONS

Bloomberg Wealth Manager - www.wealth.bloomberg.com - The trusted Bloomberg name is behind this new bimonthly magazine targeting the needs of financial planners and investment advisers who counsel the affluent. Top flight writers present key strategies and unique opportunities that are fundamental to guiding clients through everything from portfolio management, tax planning and asset protection to charitable giving and trusts.

Ticker magazine - New to the market, *Ticker* is fast becoming the magazine of choice among investment professionals. Every month it delivers strategies and state-of-the-art tools for helping financial planners, brokers, fee advisers and other financial professionals make more money for themselves as well as their clients. With today's better educated client - it's vital to stay ahead of the information curve, and *Ticker* gives financial practitioners the edge they need. Qualified planners and brokers can get a free trial subscription by calling 888-616-7676.

Registered Representative - www.rrmag.com - It's the nation's No. 1 magazine for retail stockbrokers and financial professionals, and has been named the "Best Business & Finance Magazine" by the prestigious WPA. For years, this award winning publication has been keeping the financial community up to date on the most important issues they face, as well as helping them build strong client relationships and build their practices. Featuring new books, article archives, Broker forums and other important facets, their user-friendly web site compliments the magazine itself.

Dow Jones Investment Advisor - www.djfpc.com - From the respected Dow Jones family of publications, *Investment Advisor* provides comprehensive coverage of the most vital issues affecting financial planners, broker/dealers, and money managers. Featured departments include sections on asset allocation, important books, advisor tables of funds and annuities, and more.

Financial Planning - www.fponline.com - *Financial Planning* is the official magazine of the International Association for Financial Planning. From practice management, fee adviser and compliance strategies to client and prospect development, retirement planning and general investment issues - *Financial Planning* magazine and its interactive web site bring the advising community state-of-the-art techniques and vital information for staying ahead of the game in this competitive environment.

Asset Allocation Charts

From Frontier Analytics

A Complete Client Presentation
Asset Allocation Principles

Item # T135x - 10174 $49.95

Find 20 different charts explaining the basics of Asset Allocation - perfect for making professional presentations to your clients.

Full-color slides are in the easy-to-use Microsoft PowerPoint format. Also get a complete script booklet containing bulleted discussion points and the full source of the data behind each slide. From historical performance to diversification concepts, the 20 new Frontier Asset Allocation Charts make educating clients incredibly easy.

Put it ALL at your fingertips with Frontier Analytics - and explain Asset Allocation using striking graphics, historical data and discussion points.

Adapt the presentation to your needs:

PowerPoint is so versatile, you can adapt the presentation to any format, including:

- On-Line Computer Slideshows
- Paper Flipcharts and Handouts
- Overhead Transparencies
- 35mm Slides

Charts in the set include:

- Capital Markets
- Risk/Return Relationship
- Diversification Concept
- Suitable Portfolios
- Tax Deferral, Long-Term Investing, Style Investing
- And Much More!

Item # T135x - 10174

$49.95 now $42.95 - when you call 800-511-5667 and ask for discount code T135

Order now and save 15%
Get an "FP Books" discount   800-511-5667 ext. T135

About the Author

▲　▲　▲　▲　▲

Roger C. Gibson, Chartered financial Analyst (CFA) and Certified Financial Planner (CFP), is president of Gibson Capital Management, Ltd., which provides money management services for high net worth and institutional clients nationwide.

Mr. Gibson is an internationally acclaimed expert in the field of investment policy and portfolio development. He is a sought after speaker on these topics, appearing frequently at conferences for the Securities Industry Institute, the International Association for Financial Planning. the American Institute of Certified Public Accountants and many others.

Mr. Gibson has served on the Editorial Advisory Board of the *Journal of Financial Planning* and is quoted often in respected financial publications including *The Wall Street Journal*, *Forbes, Money, Fortune* and *The New York Times.*

Money magazine has recognized Mr. Gibson as one of the top financial advisers in America, and his seminal work, the book *Asset Allocation: Balancing Financial Risk,* is widely considered to be the definitive work on the subject.

Notes

Notes

Notes

Notes

Notes

Notes